Economic Collapse Survival Manual
Author: Kambiz Mostofizadeh
Publisher: Mikazuki Publishing House
ISBN-13: 978-1-942825-05-0

Desc: Learn how to survive and thrive in an economic collapse.

INTRODUCTION

What will you do if the economy collapses and you are not prepared? Do you have the basic necessities to be able to stay alive for 6 weeks, until some form of assistance can arrive? Have you stored what you need to keep your family alive? If you were to go out today and purchase what you needed to stay alive, will you even know what to purchase? What will you do when money is no longer a valid means for trade? How will you explain to your family, that you did not spend one hour of your life preparing in case of an emergency like an economic collapse? This is not a zombie apocalypse, it is an economic collapse. That means the rules on how you conduct yourself should be different and the steps you take for your future, will be different. I hope you read and learn, because the information in this book just may save your life and the life of your loved ones.

Sincerely,
Kambiz Mostofizadeh, Author

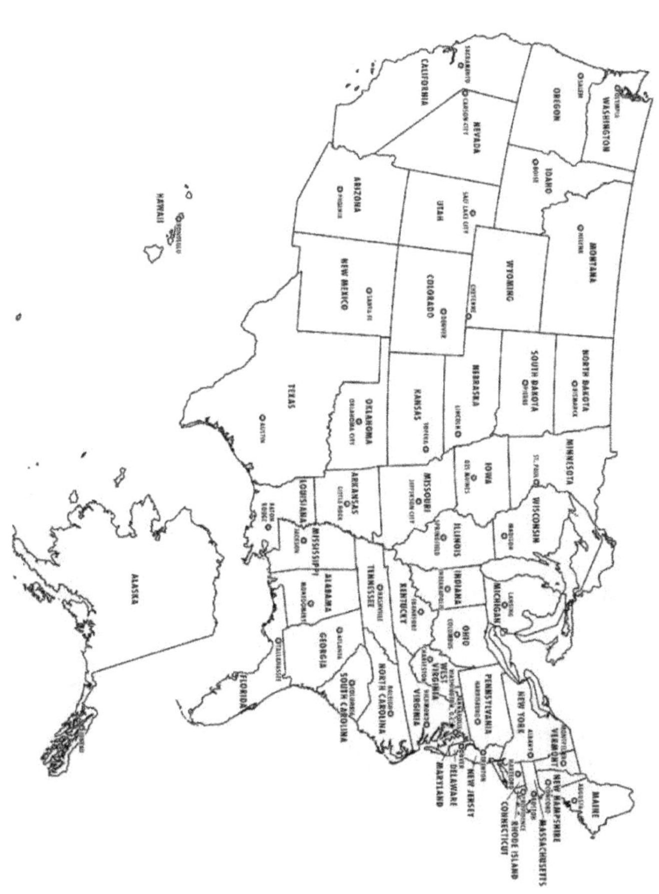

WASHINGTON
OREGON
CALIFORNIA
NEVADA
IDAHO
MONTANA
WYOMING
UTAH
ARIZONA
COLORADO
NEW MEXICO
TEXAS
OKLAHOMA
KANSAS
NEBRASKA
SOUTH DAKOTA
NORTH DAKOTA
MINNESOTA
IOWA
MISSOURI
ARKANSAS
LOUISIANA
MISSISSIPPI
ALABAMA
TENNESSEE
KENTUCKY
ILLINOIS
WISCONSIN
MICHIGAN
INDIANA
OHIO
GEORGIA
FLORIDA
SOUTH CAROLINA
NORTH CAROLINA
VIRGINIA
WEST VIRGINIA
PENNSYLVANIA
NEW YORK
VERMONT
NEW HAMPSHIRE
MAINE
MASSACHUSETTS
RHODE ISLAND
CONNECTICUT
NEW JERSEY
DELAWARE
MARYLAND
ALASKA
HAWAII

TABLE OF CONTENTS

THE WORLD IS A CHAOTIC ONE

In 2008, the world economy went in to a recession, triggered by the problems created by banks, loan brokers, and loan officers, selling predatory home loans (and their derivatives). Monetary manipulation, market manipulation, less trust in fiat currency, rising gold prices, and rising debt, assists in creating an atmosphere of uncertainty for all. War, armed conflict, and threat of constant violence is always, in one form or another, at the doorstep of humans. Because the world is chaotic and un-predictable, it is difficult to accurately forecast what will happen economically or politically. You can spend all your time worrying about what the world will do but it is much more important to focus on what you will do, if the economy does collapse again. In such a situation, your immediate neighbors will be attempting to possibly take your resources, at the point of a gun. You have to stay alive if you want to attempt to keep your family and loved ones alive. That is why the item that you should focus on is personal safety.

The world is chaotic and un-predictable.

SURVIVAL

Survival is more about a mental attitude than it is a physical one. It is your will that is fighting to survive and persevere, rather than your body. Your mind should be prepared for facing difficult situations, which is why you should use a set of principles for survival.

S – Size up the situation

U – Use all your senses

R – Remember your location

V – Vanquish all fear

I – Improvise and adapt

V – Value staying alive

A – Act like the natives and locals

L – Live by being clever

SIGNS OF EMOTIONAL IMBALANCE

(1) Hopelessness

(2) Depression or acute sadness

(3) Behavioral changes; appearance, etc.

(4) Substance abuse or alcohol abuse

(5) Risky behavioral patterns

(6) Social withdrawal

(7) Loss of hope

(8) Lack of ambition

(9) Lack of motivation

Injury, illness, and death are real possibilities a survivor has to face. Perhaps nothing is more stressful than being alone in an unfamiliar environment where you could die from hostile action, an accident, or from eating something lethal. Illness and injury can also add to stress by limiting your ability to maneuver, get food

and drink, find shelter, and defend yourself. Even if illness and injury don't lead to death, they add to stress through the pain and discomfort they generate. It is only by controlling the stress associated with the vulnerability to injury, illness, and death that you can have the courage to take
the risks associated with survival tasks. Even under the most ideal circumstances, nature is quite formidable. In survival, a soldier will have to contend with the stressors of weather, terrain, and the variety of creatures inhabiting an area. Heat, cold, rain, winds, mountains, swamps, deserts, insects, dangerous reptiles, and other animals are just a few of the challenges awaiting the soldier working to survive. Depending on how a soldier handles the stress of his environment, his surroundings can be either a source of food and protection or can be a cause of extreme discomfort leading to injury, illness, or death.

FRUGALITY

If you believe that there may be an impending economic collapse on its way, then you should adjust your lifestyle to reflect the current times. If you are already in an economic collapse, then resourcefulness is the answer. Let us imagine that you have read the news and all the experts have told you that there may be difficult economic times ahead, possibly even an economic depression. Would it not be logical for you to take immediate measures to stop the waste of money on un-important items? Every little bit of money counts and after you have saved enough, then it becomes a lot of money. But you will never save if you justify your excessive spending as being because there will be no way to effectively save up a large amount of money. If you practice the habit of frugality (spending less and not spending on un-important items), then it will become ingrained as a permanent habit that will help your future by not weighing you down financially. Everyone likes to enjoy a high standard of living or quality of living, but living within our means is priority. By living within your means and saving, you will never be lacking in essential items that you need for your happiness and survival.

GETTING FAR AWAY FROM RIOTS

Violent crowd actions can be extremely destructive to a community, resulting in burned down buildings, destruction of local economies, and dead humans. It is in your best interest to get as far away from any type of riot that you can. The only limits to violent crowd tactics are the attitude and ingenuity of crowd members, training of their leaders, and the materials available to them. Crowd or mob members may commit violent acts with crude, homemade weapons or anything else that is available. If violence is planned, crowd members may conceal makeshift weapons or tools for vandalism. Rioters can be expected to vent their emotions on individuals, authorities, and equipment. They may throw rotten fruits and vegetables, rocks, bricks, bottles, or they may direct dangerous objects (vehicles, carts, barrels, or liquids) at others. Rioters may set fire to buildings or vehicles and destroy property. In organized riots, riot leaders organize the population into quasi-military groups capable of developing plans and tactics for riots and disorders.

Riots can be instigated for:

- Theft of property/supplies as riot leaders organize a riot as a way to disrupt security surrounding logistics control points, with the objective of seizing guarded property.

- Political purpose riots are often organized for propaganda or to embarrass the government.

- Grievance protests can be organized as a riot. Under normal circumstances, this type of riot is not extremely violent in nature. It may turn violent when leaders try to exploit the successes of the riot or the weaknesses of the security force.

Unorganized riots are spontaneous, although they can be exploited and diverted by leaders into different types of riots. They are usually indicative of extreme frustration and fear. Under determined leadership, the pattern of these gatherings can change to an organized riot. Once a riot begins, it can spread to other areas and become entrenched in several different key locations. That is precisely why it is in your best interests to have pre-planned routes of escape ready in case you need to evacuate the area in case of a serious emergency like an economic collapse.

WHAT YOU SHOULD HAVE

There are a minimum amount of items that you will need, in order to ensure some form of success.

- Firearms – Varies
- Rations (Food) – Varies
- Seeds – Lettuce, Tomato, Cucumber
- Water – Varies
- 8 Person Tent - $200 to $1200
- Car with Spare Gasoline – Varies
- Compass - $8
- Solar Lantern - $20
- Solar Hand crank AM/FM/NOAA Radio - $20

- Medical Kit
- Rope
- Large Camping Backpack
- Axe
- Waterproof matches
- Water Purification Tablets
- Medications
- Tools and Supplies
- Sanitation and Hygiene
- Clothing and Bedding
- Important documents
- Sunglasses (Polarized)
- Walking Stick (retractable)
- Hiking Boots
- Warm Clothing

- Poncho

FIREARMS

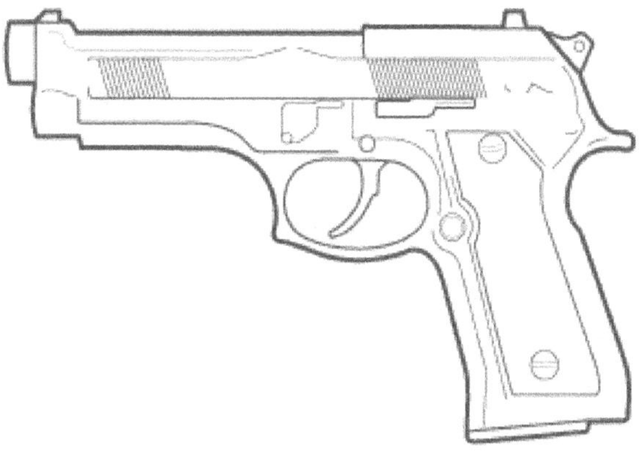

Within a few week of society experiencing a serious economic collapse, humans will resort to stealing and murdering, in order to gather the resources that they need to continue living. Is it wrong? Yes. Will people do it anyway? Yes. They will steal from one another without remorse, because staying alive and surviving is their number one priority, not being civil. Civil society has at this point broken down. People have looted shops to gather supplies. Law

Enforcement is non-existent or so dispersed, that they have little or no effectiveness. In all actuality, martial law may be declared and there will be soldiers on the streets, in order to keep security. What about your security and your family's security? That is your responsibility. So what is the best way to stay secure? You should have some form of personal weapon that is legally registered in your possession. The weapon should preferably be a handgun or rifle. If you do not have a handgun or rifle, you should attempt to find one, buy one, barter for one, or get one at any cost. If you do not have one, then you will be ordered around by people that do have one. It is as simple as that. In this situation of a serious economic collapse, you will not be able to call 911 or any phone number, for people to come and save you. You have to save yourself and you have to save your family, from being robbed, raped, or murdered.

A legally registered handgun would give you enough bullets in your clip to buy yourself enough time to get away from would-be bandits. Once you have acquired the handgun or rifle, you should spend a considerable amount of time, practicing using it. Without the training to accurately use it, you are as good as a bare-handed person.

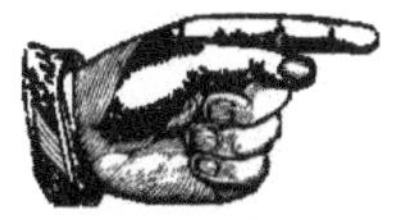

In an economic collapse, you won't be able to call 911.

In addition to the handgun or rifle, you should acquire a Bow & Arrow as well as a Knife (with a jagged edge preferably). You may run out of bullets, but arrows for your Bow can be re-used and your Knife can be used for cutting wood as well as protecting yourself. In the worst case scenario, you can make your own arrows from tree branches and rocks, giving you a virtual endless supply of arrows.

A handgun or rifle with an empty cartridge might as well be a wooden club. Also, if in the case that you do not have a projectile weapon available to you and you do not have any type of blade, then it might be in your best interest to fashion a simple club or spear and practice using them until you are able to strike with proficiency.

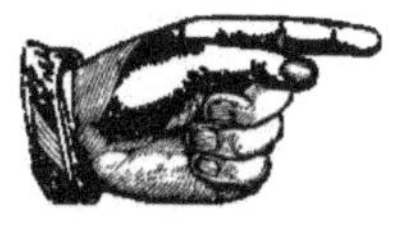

You may run out of bullets, but arrows for your bow can be re-used.

FOOD RATIONS

Food ration bars make an excellent meal for staying alive during a serious economic collapse. Each food ration bar contains between 2400 to 3600 calories, giving you the energy you will need to carry on. The amount of food rations you purchase should last you from 4 to 6 weeks. Any less than this, would be putting yourself at risk of a lack of energy that could in turn seriously hamper your productivity. If you are unable to purchase food, then you will have to move to an area that will yield food for you, like a Lake, River, Forest, or a Farm. A farm is ideal, because you can plant and grow your own food. Farms are located in areas that are at least thirty minutes away from major cities, and this will give you an advantage in security and privacy. Fishing can be done using a wooden spear or by using a piece of string with bait on it (worms make for excellent bait and they can be found in brownish-red clay dirt). In such a situation where you were lacking food, you could even dig up worms and eat them. But let us imagine that you have food rations because you took my advice and stocked up on it in case of an economic collapse. But if you did not, then you would have to fish, hunt, grow your own food, or pick fruits/vegetables/greens. If you have never fished before and you have never grown your own food before, then it might be in your best interest to hunt and pick off the trees what you can gather. You should wash and dry the plant first before eating. It should, in addition, be boiled or roasted, to kill any contaminates it contains.

Trees/Plants/Flowers You Can Eat:

Cactus
Pine Tree Needles
Dandelions
Wild Leeks
Blueberries
Bamboo (shoots)
Oak Tree (acorns)

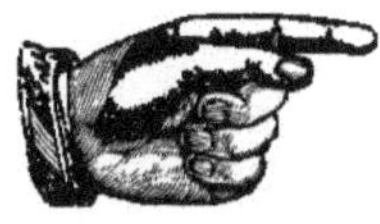

Wash, dry, and roast/boil plants that you find edible.

Because you will only be able to survive for a limited time eating wild plants and tree parts, as your digestive system is not used to this diet, you will have to view eating plants as a temporary source of nutrition. Your entire existence at this point depends on your ability to find edible food. It is better to keep moving in this situation to find more satisfactory forms of food. In addition, seeking out clean sources of water, should be as important for you as locating food. Creeks or flowing bodies of

water, should be sought out to ensure a supply of fresh water as well as to potentially access food. Life is where the water is, goes the saying. Creeks have their habitats naturally created around them and they do attract animals that are seeking to drink water. If you start farming on a land you find (whether near a creek or not), then you will be forced to stay in that location until your food grows to the size that it is edible. That may take a long time and the possibility that you will, at least once, be approached by bandits (there could be more than one), goes up substantially. By moving constantly, you will be able to better understand where the high yield and low yield lands are for finding food. Moving constantly will also prevent the danger of being overtaken at night (or in the day) by robbers seeking your supplies. Although humanity should seek to comfort each other in times of danger, it can be said with certainty that when a serious

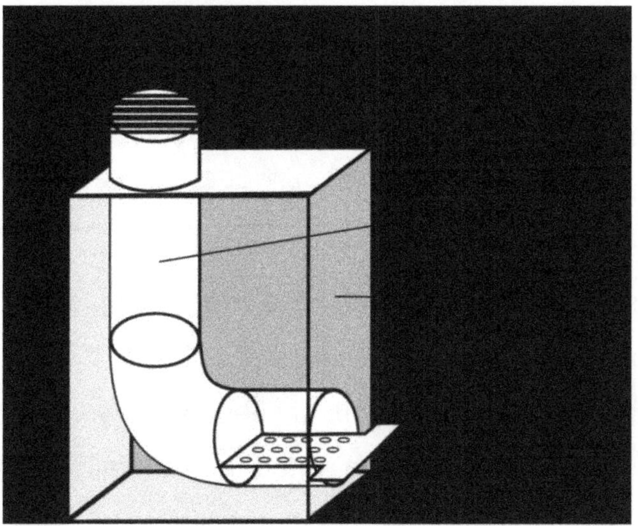

economic collapse occurs in the United States and law enforcement is non-existent, humans will rob and steal from one another in order to ensure their survival. Therefore, you should not share with others from where your food is supplied nor from where it is being replenished. If you share this with them, you stand the chance of being murdered by bandits that have the hope of taking what you own. That is what your firearms are for, to protect you and your supplies in such situations. Your food is an item that is more valuable than anything you have. Rationing your food is vital to your survival so you should only use as much of your food supply that you need to survive. This is not a time for gluttony and over-eating to soak the pain of the economic collapse. It is the time to re-build your shelter, gather your food and store it, save water, to eventually seek out signs of the existence of other humans. Hunting in this situation, may be your best bet for staying alive until some type of help arrives. The two best ways to hunt are by setting traps or by using a weapon to catch your game. Traps are not that difficult to make, but the wait until an animal arrives will test your nerves, and may result in no animal showing up. In this case, an attitude of being pro-active will assist you in hunting and catching game. The forests contain various wildlife that can be eaten and the animals that are actually available for you to hunt will be based on your location.

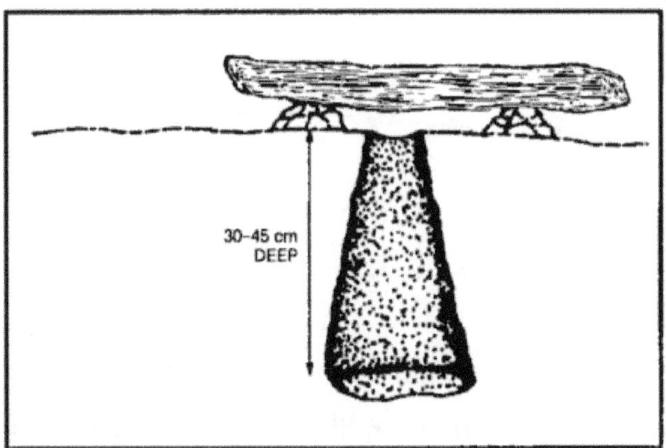

The easiest trap to make is a deadfall. Dig a hole, about 3-6 feet deep, and then cover it with tree parts and branches, so that it seems natural. An animal that falls in to the deadfall will be your next meal. You can dramatically raise your chances of catching food by building more than one deadfall, one preferably near where you are camped and one in the forest. Another way to build a simple trap is to put branches together in the form of a shoe box. The trap should be put together in a way that it will not fall apart. Lift up one end of the trap and place a half foot stick under it, so there is

room for the animal to enter under the trap. Attach a rope to the half foot stick and wait at a distance for an animal to crawl in to the trap box. Once the animal does, pull the rope and the box will trap the animal inside. You now have your meal. The third method for hunting is as effective as it is ancient. Break off a 5 foot long branch, that is at least one inch in thickness, and then sharpen both ends of it, until it is sharp enough to stab tree bark. Now you have a fashionable weapon to hunt larger game. If you climb a tree about 3 meters high,

you will have enough of a view to be able to see all around you. The human eye is capable of seeing up to 200 kilometers, and the elevated tree view will greatly ease the difficulty in finding game.

If you are able to catch enough food, you can use the food to barter with other humans for items that you need. In this type situation, food is more valuable to you than money is. In this situation, food is money. It does not matter what method you use to find food, you should know that the pre-occupation with finding food, will be the majority of your activity during the collapse.

FISHING TIPS

Do not eat fish that appears spoiled. Cooking does not ensure that spoiled fish will be edible. Signs of spoilage are:-

• Sunken eyes.

• Peculiar odor.

• Suspicious color. (Gills should be red to pink. Scales should be a pronounced shade of gray, not faded.)

• Dents stay in the fish's flesh after pressing it with your thumb.

• Slimy, rather than moist or wet body.

• Sharp or peppery taste.

MONEY IN THE BANK

"I reached my hand down and picked it up; it made my heart thump, for I was certain it was gold."
- James Marshall, 1848

According to Forbes magazine, the United States is the largest holder of Gold reserves in the world with 8,133.5 tons. But where did it begin? The Gold Rush in California started when James Marshall in January 24, 1848 discovered Gold nugget while building a sawmill in California. The news of his discovery spread like wildfire and the Gold Rush began, sparking a huge wave of migrants and immigrants to the West looking for Gold. Up until 100 years ago, gold was used as the medium of exchange in America, despite the existence of paper money. Money may become worthless during an economic collapse and the medium of exchange may be other forms of currency including food, water, shelter, etc. Central Banks buy gold to add to their reserves as a defense against the volatility of international markets. Gold, although not known for exceedingly high returns, has historically been a safe investment for banks, governments, and even corporations. During an economic collapse, everyone will be trying to access their bank

account at the bank branch which they use. There may be possible riots and/or angry crowds blocking the front of the bank. In such a situation, you will face very heavy lines, possible security/police presence, and unruly customers that want their money just as bad as you do. If you convert 1/3rd of your disposable income every month to purchasing gold (from whoever your heart desires), then you will have a greater sense of security. That gold will accumulate and since no one can predict with any certainty when the economic collapse occur, your gold will be your 'nest egg' and your savings. If no economic collapse ever occurs in your lifetime, then all that will have happened is that you will saved a lot of gold that can be converted in to paper money anytime that you wish. It is better to be safe in this situation, than being sorry. Being safe and secure means having enough gold saved up so if an economic collapse does occur, you can be comforted in the fact that you have saved. What type of gold should you purchase and how will I know if it is really gold that I am buying? You should only buy gold from credible sources that have some type of track record or history of successfully serving customers. The type of gold available for purchase varies from 10K, 14K, 18K, 22K, and 24K. Gold is an asset and in many nations on earth, such as India, you can take your gold jewelry in to a bank and be paid interest on your gold. Some banks pay up to 2 percent or more, depending on the length in which you deposit the gold. You are in effect monetizing un-used gold that is lying in your dresser drawer and receiving interest for having deposited in the bank. Once the period in which you have deposited the gold finishes, you are free to take your gold. You made money off gold that was not being used and your gold appreciated making you money from both. It is a win-win situation.

MAKING MONEY DURING THE COLLAPSE

How on earth can I make money during the collapse? Firstly, it would be understanding and identifying the key resources that will rise in value and the resources that may become useless. First off, let us discuss the items that will become useless and the principle of "traveling light". The items that will be useless are items like paper money, diamonds, expensive watches, one thousand dollar pairs of shoes, and lava lamps. The items that will become highly valuable are items like water, food, extra or spare rifle/handguns, rope, agricultural seeds, maps, solar radios, and extra tools that you can barter with. You will be able to barter (I give you this and you give me that!) for items that you need by having bought beforehand items that you can use to barter with. The barter system is an ancient system that has proven itself in being able to meet the needs of society. So how can you grow more prosperous in such a system? By having more items to trade. The more items that you possess, the more items you have to trade, and this translates directly in to economic power during the collapse. The problem is that you can only be able to protect a certain amount of what you own. The rest you will not be able to adequately protect because you may be lacking in "strength of numbers" to do so. This is why you should seek to join, cooperate, and re-form a community, in the case of the collapse. If each person is just out for themselves, then the entire system will implode. Humans have to depend on each other to do the right thing, for the general welfare and safety of all. Also by joining together with other individuals (even if solely for economic reasons), then you have comfort in knowing that there are more than one of you, working for survival.

There is strength
In numbers.

WATER IS LIFE

Water is among the most important items for your existence because up to 75 percent of your body is comprised of water. Conservation of your water supply is vital to your existence therefore your water should be both stored and hidden from potential robbers. Water can be gathered and traded for other essential items as well as being used for cooking purposes. You can use multiple methods to find water.

Up to 75 percent of
your body is water.

The easiest method to find water is to seek out a clean water source like a lake, creek, river or any moving body of water. Dehydration is a matter that must be dealt with by constantly finding new sources of water for replenishment. You may be able to survive for three days without food, but if you are unable to drink water, you may die or severely damage your brain. In the early morning, say 5am to 6am, the condensation of water in the form of dew, can be collected on plastic or reflective materials. Any water you collect should be boiled, strained, or filtered. If you find yourself without water, digging a hole 1 to 2 feet deep may reveal some water that has to be strained.

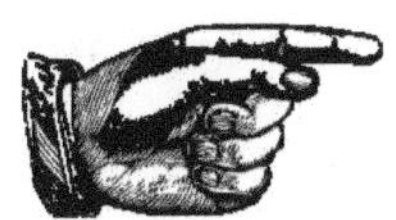

Drink a liter of water per day.

Because water is moving down from a mountain, then water can be found by moving to lower areas. Constantly moving water will be drinkable water, as it is safe. Slow moving water will form algae and bacteria that is very harmful if drank. Water should be, at the very minimum, boiled. And if you are unable to boil it right at that point, then you should use water purification tablets inside of a water container to do so. Drinking contaminated water will harm your body and may cause you diarrhea, which can be potentially deadly when you lack the adequate medical supplies to remedy it. Water is not only an essential item for your survival but it is also a needed item to barter with. If you spend time for gathering water, you will have security in having an ample supply of water as well as having the satisfaction of being able to barter excess water that you have so that you can acquire essential items that you need.

Water flows downward.

Dehydration results from inadequate replacement of lost body fluids. It decreases your efficiency and, if injured, increases your susceptibility to severe shock. Consider the following results of body fluid loss:

• A 5 percent loss of body fluids results in thirst, irritability, nausea, and weakness.

• A 10 percent loss results in dizziness, headache, inability to walk, and a tingling sensation in the limbs.

• A 15 percent loss results in dim vision, painful urination, swollen tongue, deafness, and a numb feeling in the skin.

• A loss greater than 15 percent of body fluids may result in death.

CREATING A PROPER FIRE

Let's hope that you were smart enough to purchase waterproof matches beforehand because you listened to my advice. So now you are in a forest during an economic collapse and it is getting rather cold. You decide to build a fire to warm your body and to cook your food. What is the best route to take? Creating a proper fire starts with understanding the principle behind building a fire. The fire is built in stages and over time, not at once. First, you should dig a fire pit hole to hold the fire. The fire pit should be large enough to accommodate the wood you will burn. Around the fire pit hole, you should place large rocks to prevent fiery ashes from escaping and causing brush fires. First, you should gather thin strips of burnable dry wood like tree bark and use this as the tinder. Using the waterproof matches, light the tree bark and place it in the fire pit. Now you will start placing small twigs of wood on top of the bark. Now start placing slightly larger pieces of wood. Continue this process until enough hot coals have been created allowing you to place a thick wooden log on the fire pit.

LEAVING OR STAYING?

Let us say that you are lucky to enough to see other people. Do you help them or avoid them? In such a time it is safe to assume that everyone will be, for the most part, attempting to rob and possibly even, kill each other to ensure their own survival. What if they (the community you join) decide collectively to rob you? Or decides collectively to kill you? Or decides collectively to imprison you? In such a situation where civil society has broken down, there is no reason to believe that humans will do the right thing. There is no appeals court. There may not even be a jury. The prosecutor, judge, and jury, in such a situation, may be the same. There is no guarantee that there will be anything resembling legal justice, when a serious economic collapse occurs. Being within a community that contains many resources can of course help you greatly but it is important to note that any such community during a serious economic collapse would become the target for robbers, bandits, and thieves of all sorts. In such a time, it could be to retreat to the safety of the mountains. Mountains have natural shelter in the form of trees, are difficult to reach by robbers, and give you a natural advantage by being able to see danger as it approaches from a far distance. Higher elevations have always naturally created safety and mountains contain wildlife that could serve as food for you.

Higher elevations are safer.

EVACUATING THE CITY

There may be conditions under which you will decide to get away or there may be situations when you are ordered to leave. Plan places where your family will meet, both within and outside of your immediate neighborhood. Use the Family Emergency Plan to decide these locations before a disaster. If you have a car, keep a full tank of gas in it if an evacuation seems likely. Keep a half tank of gas in it at all times in case of an unexpected need to evacuate. Gas stations may be closed during emergencies and unable to pump gas during power outages. Plan to take one car per family to reduce congestion and delay. Become familiar with alternate routes and other means of transportation out of your area. Choose several destinations in different directions so you have options in an emergency. Leave early enough to avoid being trapped by severe weather.

Follow recommended evacuation routes. Do not take shortcuts; they may be blocked.

Be alert for road hazards such as washed-out roads or bridges and downed power lines. Do not drive into flooded areas. If you do not have a car, plan how you will leave if you have to. Make arrangements with family, friends or your local government. Take your emergency supply kit unless you have reason to believe it has been contaminated. Listen to a battery-powered radio and follow local evacuation instructions. Take your pets with you, but understand that only service animals may be permitted in public shelters. Plan how you will care for your pets in an emergency. Call or email the out-of-state contact in your family communications plan and tell them where you are going. Secure your home by closing and locking doors and windows and unplug electrical equipment such as radios, televisions and small appliances. Leave freezers and refrigerators plugged in unless there is a risk of flooding.

If there is damage to your home and you are instructed to do so, shut off water, gas and electricity before leaving. Leave a note telling others when you left and where you are going. Wear sturdy shoes and clothing that provides some protection such as long pants, long-sleeved shirts and a cap. Check with neighbors who may need a ride.

Once you have moved into the area in which you want to hide (hide area), select a hide site. Keep the following formula in mind when selecting a hide site:

B.L.I.S.S.

B - Blends in with the surroundings.

L - Low in silhouette.

I - Irregular in shape.

S - Small in size.

S - Secluded.

- Avoid the use of existing buildings or shelters.
- Usually, your best option will be to crawl into the thickest vegetation you can find.
- Construct any type of shelter within the hide area only in cold weather and desert environments.
- If you build a shelter, follow the BLISS formula.

PITCHING TENT

When you are in a survival situation and realize that shelter is a high priority, start looking for shelter as soon as possible. As you do so, remember what you will need at the site. Two requisites are:

- It must contain material to make the type of shelter you need.

- It must be large enough and level enough for you to lie down comfortably.

Before setting up your shelter, first take one hour to remove all the debris, rock, and various items in the area in which you wish to set up your shelter. Rocks can be a painful surprise on the ground when turning in your sleep, if you have not previously prepared the ground in which you setup your shelter on.

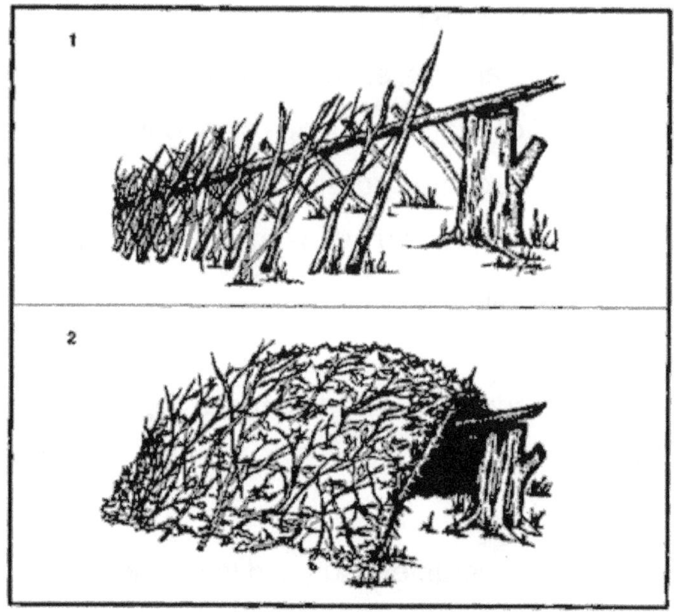

Simple Debris Hut pictured above

You must also consider whether the site:

- Provides concealment from observation.
- Has escape routes.
- Is suitable for signaling

- Provides protection against wild animals and rocks and dead trees that might fall.

- Is free from insects, reptiles, and poisonous plants.

You must also remember the problems that could arise in your environment.

- Avoid flash flood areas in foothills.

- Avoid avalanche or rockslide areas in mountainous terrain.

- Avoid sites near bodies of water that are below the high water mark.

The fastest and easiest way to create shelter is to break a thin tree from the middle of it base about 36 inches high, while leaving it connected. The tree branch is laid down to the ground with it still being connected. A vinyl

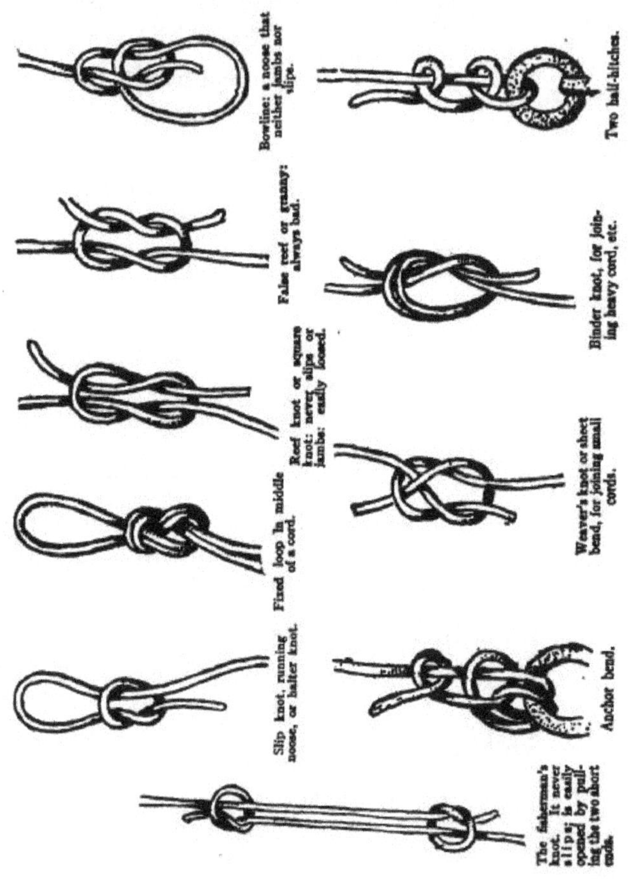

blanket or tarp is laid over the branch so that the middle of the branch is running through the middle of the blanket, covering both sides of the branch creating a tent. Trees provide a natural shelter even if you did not have a tent, but a tent is important because it keeps away animals, critters, and other wildlife.

Trees give you a natural shelter.

The elevated treehouse tent made by Tentsile, is a great investment, because it gives you the advantage of pitching tent between two trees on an elevated position, which gives you both views in all directions as well as the advantage of security. If you do not have a professional tent and you don't want to break a tree to pitch a tent, then you can find 5 or 6 foot long broken tree branches and lean them against a large tree until you have a simple structure. After this simple structure of multiple 5 foot branches is laid against a large tree, the top of the branches is covered with tree shrubs, light branches, and other natural covering you can find to fill the top. Once the top of your structure is filled, you should create a doorway by moving one of the branches at the far corner of your structure.

Elevated tents are safer

HUMANS WILL GO CANNIBAL

Rapidly rising food prices in an economic collapse will mean that food may only be available to certain individuals. A large portion of the population will starve to death or resort to cannibalism (eating other humans). After one month of being without food that they are used to, they may resort to eating each other and selling each other, in order to eat. Humans could go as far as creating human ranches to have a stable supply of food. Food production of cattle and vegetables will slow down to nearly nil in the first six weeks of the economic collapse and humans killing humans with the purpose of eating them will become a widespread phenomenon. Although a human can survive on human meat (what a horrible notion!!!), it is not only undesirable but the long term effects of such diet could have serious health consequences. Keeping your family safe and secure should be your most important priority at such at time and it is hard to imagine that under such a stressful situation, you now have to fend off humans that are seeking to eat you.

Cannibalism in America has a long and rich history, dating back to the early settlers that crossed in caravans from the East Coast to the West. In 1846, the Donner Party, George and Jacob Donner, were part of the wave of settlers that crossed the Oregon Trail in to Nevada.

Although there has been no concrete evidence presented of their cannibalism, the Donner Party is a legend among storytellers that contains hints of truth in it. It has not been proven that the Donner Party ate anything other than a rat, their dog, or a leather belt, but the campsites of the settlers not associated with the Donner Party, shows signs of human cannibalism having taken place. During a harsh winter, where supplies are running out rapidly, the lack of food will make humans that would not normally eat other humans begin to question themselves. Would you rather starve or survive? What if you had to choose to eat someone because you are starving? Would you starve to death or would you do the inconceivable act of eat another human. Many humans will choose to survive and their survival will cause humans to be eaten. What will happen when individuals that are used to receiving food stamps to survive, stop receiving them? What will happen when banks are closed and money is worthless? People will become scared and their first reaction will be to panic while thinking about what they need to survive. In that situation, you do not have time to think about what you will do. You should have planned beforehand what you need to do if such a situation occurs. What will happen when humans are facing the potentially life threatening situation of being without food and they lack the survival skills (hunting, fishing, gathering, etc.) to capture food? Will they see humans as an easier method for gastronomic satisfaction in contrast to going through the painstakingly difficult methods of hunting, fishing, and gathering? Let us hope not but all the trends point to such a situation. In this scenario, it would be best to avoid contact with humans, not only to avoid becoming, but to avoid turning to cannibalism in packs. You can survive by knowing basic fishing, hunting, and gathering techniques, without having to resort to gut wrenching methods such as cannibalism. If the Donner Party survived the harsh winter of 1846 by eating a dog and their own leather belts, then you can survive on less calorie intake. How can you be prepared for a time that you will intake less calories? By making it a regular routine to consume less calories, you will train your body to become used to taking in less calories. Having fat can be useful when you are in a near starving condition, but excess fat will slow you down and tire you out during movement. If an economic collapse occurs where less food intake is the norm, is it not wise to start by taking less food from today?

Humans will resort to eating each other after 6 weeks in an economic collapse.

FINDING AUTHORITY

As The Posse Comitatus Act prohibits the use of federal forces for any direct civil law enforcement activities, the National Guard will most likely be the authority attempting to restore civil society and civil infrastructure. The 49th MP Brigade (National Guard) provided civil disturbance assistance to Los Angeles in the aftermath of the Rodney King trial.

It will be in your interest to constantly have knowledge of what is happening in your immediate and distant surroundings. The use of your Solar Powered Radio will allow you to hear broadcasts that may give you a location on where to come to for help. According to the FCC, the Early Warning System is a national public warning system that requires TV and radio broadcasters, cable television systems, wireless cable systems, satellite digital audio radio service providers, direct broadcast satellite service providers and wireline video service providers to offer to the President the communications capability to address the American public. The frequency 40.5 Megahertz (MHz) is designated as the military joint common frequency. Frequencies 167.0875 MHz and 414.0375 MHz are designated by the U.S. Army as National Calling Channels for initial contact with law enforcement agencies. In such a time of an economic collapse, the only authorities remaining may be a hodgepodge collection of law enforcement, city and State officials, as well as Federal officers. It is important to know where they are and how to get in contact with them. The goal of authorities in such a situation should be that of promoting collectivism, safety, hope, peace, and progress.

EWS is a public warning system.

AIR TO GROUND SIGNALING

There may be a chance that you will see an airplane or helicopter approaching your location. By creating the symbols on the ground, you can signal the airplane or helicopter from a distance.

V – Need Assistance

X – Need Medical Assistance

N – No or negative

Y – Yes or affirmative

🡅 - Follow this direction

Air to ground signals allow airplanes and helicopters to see you.

The ground to air symbols should be made large enough so that an airplane or helicopter could easily see it from a distance and higher elevation. Wood, debris, and even brush, can be used to form the ground to air signals.

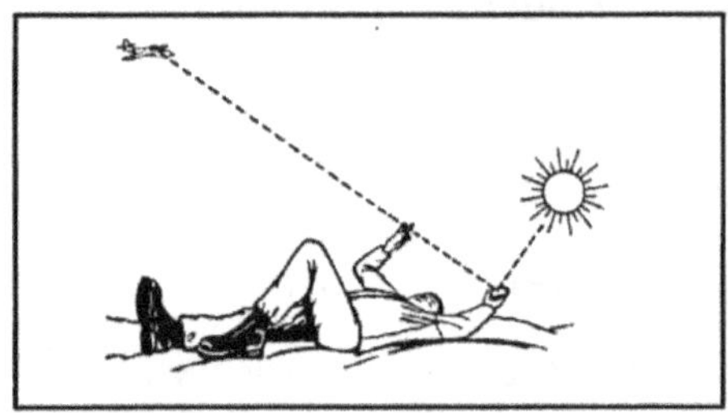

Another method for signaling is to use a mirror to reflect the sun's rays towards the airplane or helicopter. In order to do so, you should lay down on the ground and aim the light towards the cockpit.

During darkness, fire is the most effective visual means for signaling. Build three fires in a triangle (the international distress signal) or in a straight line with about 25 meters between the fires. Build them as soon as time and the situation permit and protect them until you need them. If you are alone, maintaining three fires may be difficult. If so, maintain one signal fire. When constructing signal fires, consider your geographic location. If in a jungle, find a natural clearing or the edge of a stream where you can build fires that the jungle foliage will not hide. You may even have to clear an area. If in a snow-covered area, you may have to clear the ground of snow or make a platform on which to build the fire so that melting snow will not extinguish it.

A burning tree (tree torch) is another way to attract attention. You can set pitch-bearing trees afire, even when green. You can get other types of trees to burn by placing dry wood in the lower branches and igniting it so that the flames flare up and ignite the foliage. Before the primary tree is consumed, cut and add more small green trees to the fire to produce more smoke. Always select an isolated tree so that you do not start a forest fire and endanger yourself.

Smoke

During daylight, build a smoke generator and use smoke to gain attention. The international distress signal is three columns of smoke. Try to create a color of smoke that contrasts with the background; dark smoke against a light background and vice versa. If you practically smother a large fire with green leaves, moss, or a little water, the fire will produce white smoke. If you add rubber or oil-soaked rags to a fire, you will get black smoke.

MINDSTATE DURING THE COLLAPSE

Your mind state during the collapse should be calm, collected, flexible, enduring, hopeful, positive, and stress-free. It is perfectly normal to experience higher than normal frustration during an economic collapse. Frustration leads to guilt and stress related effects can be life threatening during such a sensitive time. You have to be dynamic in the understanding that nothing is in your control. Even the things you think are in your control, you cannot control. You can only control yourself and you can only make decisions for yourself. The name of the game is survival and the point of this entire exercise is for you to have some preparedness if an economic collapse does occur. There are certain principles that will help you survive and thrive in such a situation and these are frugality, resourcefulness, and being dynamic. Frugality means you save what you have and do not squander or waste anything. Resourcefulness means to make the best use of what you currently have. Being dynamic means moving forward in progression, however slow. If you are alone in a forest attempting to survive, boredom and melancholy may begin to affect you. Keeping busy and constantly engaged is the key to averting boredom. In such a situation, you would barely have time to rest because all of your time would be engaged in building/upgrading shelter, hunting/gathering food, finding/storing water, and finding resources to barter.

FINDING RESOURCES

The last thing that you would want to during an economic collapse is to steal and rob from your fellow humans. That is why it is essential that you understand what the resources are that will be vital if the economic collapse occurs.

Wood sap is excellent glue.

Paper money will most likely be worthless and valueless during an economic collapse. The main resources you should gather are:

(Listed in no particular order)

a. Water
b. Food

c. Wood
d. Precious metals

Water is probably the most valuable resource and it should be discovered, stored, and traded in a Barter transaction for other items that you need. Food, because of its highly perishable nature, can be only be found and eaten or traded, immediately after being hunted/gathered. Wood can be gathered (dead wood) from the floor or taken from a tree and stored for later use. Wood will fuel your fires to cook your meals, will keep you warm at night, and can serve as a signaling aid in case of rescue. Wood sap can also provide glue for binding together items as well as providing the base for the creation of game hunting weapons like spears and Bow & Arrows. Precious metals will be seen as valuable items to be used in industrial purposes as well as medicinal purposes. Silver is known to kill germs which are something that will be rampant, during such a time. It is important to focus on the four resources of water, food, wood, and precious metals. Once you have an ample supply of these, you can trade them to receive items that can assist you.

FLOATING IN WATER

If the water is warm enough for swimming and you do not have the time or materials to construct a raft, you can use various flotation devices to negotiate the body of water. Some items you can use for flotation devices are

• Trousers - Knot each trouser leg at the bottom and close the fly. With both hands, grasp the waistband at the sides and swing the trousers in the air to trap air in each leg. Quickly press the sides of the waistband together and hold it underwater so that the air will not escape. You now have water wings to keep you afloat as you cross the body of water. Wet the trousers before inflating to trap the air better. You may have to inflate the trousers several times when crossing a large body of water.

• Empty containers - Lash together her empty gas cans, water jugs, ammo cans, boxes, or other items that will trap or hold air. Use them as water wings. Use this type of flotation device only in a slow-moving river or stream.

• Plastic bags and ponchos - Fill two or more plastic bags with air and secure them together at the opening. Use your poncho and roll green vegetation tightly inside it so that you have a roll at least 20 centimeters in diameter. Tie the ends of the roll securely. You can wear it around your waist or across one shoulder and under the opposite arm.

Logs - Use a stranded drift log if one is available, or find a log near the water to use as a float. Be sure to test the log before starting to cross. Some tree logs, palm for example, will sink even when the wood is dead. Another method is to tie two logs about 60 centimeters apart. Sit between the logs with your back against one and your legs over the other

Cattails - Gather stalks of cattails and tie them in a bundle 25 centimeters or more in diameter. The many air cells in each stalk cause a stalk to float until it rots. Test the cattail bundle to be sure it will support your weight before trying to cross a body of water.

FINDING DIRECTION

The earth's relationship to the sun can help you to determine direction on earth. The sun always rises in the east and sets in the west, but not exactly due east or due west. There is also some seasonal variation. In the northern hemisphere, the sun will be due south when at its highest point in the sky, or when an object casts no appreciable shadow. In the southern hemisphere, this same noonday sun will mark due north. In the northern hemisphere, shadows will move clockwise. Shadows will move counterclockwise in the southern hemisphere. With practice, you can use shadows to determine both direction and time of day. The shadow methods used for direction finding are the shadow-tip and watch methods.

Shadow-Tip Method

In the first shadow-tip method, find a straight stick 1 meter long, and a level spot free of brush on which the stick will cast a definite shadow. This method is simple and accurate and consists of four steps:

• Step 1. Place the stick or branch into the ground at a level spot where it will cast a distinctive shadow. Mark the shadow's tip with a stone, twig, or other means. This first shadow mark is always west-everywhere on earth.

• Step 2. Wait 1 to 1 5 minutes until the shadow tip moves a few centimeters. Mark the shadow tip's new position in the same way as the first.

• Step 3. Draw a straight line through the two marks to obtain an approximate east-west line.

• Step 4. Stand with the first mark (west) to your left and the second mark to your right, you are now facing north. This fact is true everywhere on earth.

IMPROVISED COMPASS

You can construct improvised compasses using a piece of ferrous metal that can be needle shaped or a flat double-edged razor blade and a piece of nonmetallic string or long hair from which to suspend it. You can magnetize or polarize the metal by slowly stroking it in one direction on a piece of silk or carefully through your hair using deliberate strokes. You can also polarize metal by stroking it repeatedly at one end with a magnet. Always rub in one direction only. If you have a battery and some electric wire, you can polarize the metal electrically. The wire should be insulated. If not insulated, wrap the metal object in a single, thin strip of paper to prevent contact. The battery must be a minimum of 2 volts. Form a coil with the electric wire and touch its ends to the battery's terminals. Repeatedly insert one end of the metal object in and out of the coil. The needle will become an electromagnet. When suspended from a piece of nonmetallic string, or floated on a small piece of wood in water, it will align itself with a north-south line. You can construct a more elaborate improvised compass using a sewing needle or thin metallic object, a nonmetallic container (for example, a plastic dip container), its lid with the center cut out and waterproofed, and the silver tip from a pen. To construct this compass, take an ordinary sewing needle and break in half. One half will form your direction pointer and the other will act as the pivot point. Push the portion used as the pivot point through the bottom center of your container; this portion should be flush on the bottom and not interfere with the lid. Attach the center of the other portion (the pointer) of the needle on the pen's silver tip using glue, tree sap, or melted plastic. Magnetize one end of the pointer and rest it on the pivot point.

FINDING NORTH

It may be that you are in a position that you are without a compass or any direction finding device. Finding the North Star will allow you to find your direction when travelling at night. Throughout history, the North Star has allowed sailors and marine navigators find their bearing. Because the place of the stars in the sky move according to the time of day or night and location, you will have to wait until it is night, so that you can attempt to locate the direction finding North Star. The North Star is located between the Big Dipper (large cooking pot shaped constellation) and Cassiopeia. By locating the Big Dipper, you can find the North Star. The Big Dipper is located across from the North Star and by following the edge of the Big Dipper you can find the bright glowing North Star. Once you have found the North Star, you will have definitive proof of the direction of

North, allowing you to make decisions for your travel.

MOVEMENT

Anything that shines automatically attracts attention and will give away your location. Whenever possible, wash oily skin and reapply camouflage. Skin oil will wash off camouflage, so reapply it frequently. If you must wear glasses, camouflage them by applying a thin layer of dust to the outside of the lenses. This layer of dust will reduce the reflection of light. Cover shiny spots on equipment by painting, covering with mud, or wrapping with cloth or tape. Pay particular attention to covering boot eyelets, buckles on equipment, watches and jewelry, zippers, and uniform insignia. Carry a signal mirror in its designed pouch or in a pocket with the mirror portion facing your body.

Shadow

When hiding or traveling, stay in the deepest part of the shadows. The outer edges of the shadows are lighter and the deeper parts are darker. Remember, if you are in an area where there is plenty of vegetation; keep as much vegetation between you and a potential enemy as possible. This action will make it very hard for the enemy to see you as the vegetation will partially mask you from his view. Forcing an enemy to look through many layers of masking vegetation will fatigue his eyes very quickly. When traveling, especially in built-up areas at night, be aware of where you cast your shadow. It may extend out around the comer of a building and give away your position. Also, if you are in a dark shadow and there is a light source to one side, an enemy on the other side can see your silhouette against the light.

Movement

Movement, especially fast movement, attracts attention. If at all possible, avoid movement in the presence of an enemy. If capture appears imminent in your present location and you must move, move away slowly, making as little noise as possible. By moving slowly in a survival situation, you decrease the chance of detection and conserve energy that you may need for long-term survival or long-distance evasion.

When moving past obstacles, avoid going over them. If you must climb over an obstacle, keep your body level with its top to avoid silhouetting yourself. Do not silhouette yourself against the skyline when crossing hills or ridges. When you are moving, you will have difficulty detecting the movement of others. Stop frequently, listen, and look around slowly to detect signs of hostile movement.

Noise

Noise attracts attention, especially if there is a sequence of loud noises such as several snapping twigs. If possible, avoid making any noise at all. Slow down your pace as much as necessary to avoid making noise when moving around or away from possible threats. Use background noises to cover the noise of your movement. Sounds of aircraft, trucks, generators, strong winds, and people talking will cover some or all the sounds produced by your movement. Rain will mask a lot of movement noise, but it also reduces your ability to detect potential enemy noise.

Scent

Whether hunting animals or avoiding the enemy, it is always wise to camouflage the scent associated with humans. Start by washing yourself and your clothes without using soap. This washing method removes soap and body odors. Avoiding strong smelling foods, such as garlic, helps reduce body odors. Do not use tobacco products, candy, gum, or cosmetics. You can use aromatic herbs or plants to wash yourself and your clothing, to rub on your body and clothing, or to chew on to camouflage your breath. Pine needles, mint, or any similar aromatic plant will help camouflage your scent from both animals and humans. Standing in smoke from a fire can help mask your scent from animals. While animals are afraid of fresh smoke from a fire, older smoke scents are normal smells after forest fires and do not scare them.

While traveling, use your sense of smell to help you find or avoid humans. Pay attention to smells associated with humans, such as fire, cigarettes, gasoline, oil, soap, and food. Such smells may alert you to their presence long before you can see or hear them, depending on wind speed and direction. Note the wind's direction and, when possible, approach from or skirt around on the downwind side when nearing humans or animals.

METHODS OF MOVEMENT

Sometimes you need to move, undetected, to or from a location. You need more than just camouflage to make these moves successfully. The ability to stalk or move without making any sudden quick movement or loud noise is essential to avoiding detection. You must practice stalking if it is to be effective. Use the following techniques when practicing.

Upright Movement

Take steps about half your normal stride when stalking in the upright position. Such strides help you to maintain your balance. You should be able to stop at any point in that movement and hold that position as long as necessary.

Curl the toes up out of the way when stepping down so the outside edge of the ball of the foot touches the ground. Feel for sticks and twigs that may snap when you place your weight on them. If you start to step on one, lift your foot and move it. After making contact with the outside edge of the ball of your foot, roll to the inside ball of your foot, place your heel down, followed by your toes. Then gradually shift your weight forward to the front foot. Lift the back foot to about knee height and start the process over again.

Keep your hands and arms close to your body and avoid waving them about or hitting vegetation. When moving in a crouch, you gain extra support by placing your hands on your knees. One step usually takes 1 minute to complete, but the time it takes will depend on the situation.

Crawling

Crawl on your hands and knees when the vegetation is too low to allow you to walk upright without being seen. Move one limb at a time and be sure to set it down softly, feeling for anything that may snap and make noise. Be careful that your toes and heels do not catch on vegetation.

Prone

To stalk in the prone position, you do a low, modified push-up on your hands and toes, moving yourself forward slightly, and then lowering yourself again slowly. Avoid dragging and scraping along the ground as this makes excessive noise and leaves large trails for trackers to follow.

FINDING NEW HORIZONS

It may occur that you may be unable to stay in the United States during an economic collapse. In this case, let us imagine that, you decide to leave for Canada or Mexico. In such a situation, travel will be more dangerous than during normal times. The likelihood that there will be bandits and robbers in your path is high. The probability that the roads you travel will be littered with abandoned cars is also high. Because travel, during an economic collapse, will be highly difficult, you should follow some safety principles when travelling. Travelling at night has the advantage of allowing you to cloak yourself in the darkness of the night. It would also be in your best interests, not to move on known roads. Travelling off road, in such a situation, will be your best option for leaving the United States safely. You may have to cross the border in to Canada and Mexico, and it is very likely that you will not be the only one that has had this idea. If an economic collapse occurs in the United States, that causes Americans to flee in to Canada or Mexico, the probability that the borders of these two nations will be protected or guarded is also high. In this case, you will have to watch the border for at least 24 hours before crossing, so that you have an idea of when the border guards come and go, so that your border crossing will not be noticed. The rule during such travel is above all, travel light. Only take items that will ensure your survival (water, food, etc.) and discard any items that will weigh you down, ultimately slowing you down. Crossing the border in to Canada or in to Mexico, will allow you to reach greater access to resources that ensure your survival, like water and food.

CONTACT WITH LOCALS

You must give serious consideration to dealing with the local people. Do they have a primitive culture? Are they farmers, fishermen, friendly people, or enemy? As a survivor, "cross-cultural communication" can vary radically from area to area and from people to people. It may mean interaction with people of an extremely primitive culture or contact with people who have a relatively modem culture. A culture is identified by standards of behavior that its members consider proper and acceptable but may or may not conform to your idea of what is proper. No matter who these people are, you can expect they will have laws, social and economic values, and political and religious beliefs that may be radically different from yours. Before deploying into your area of operations, study these different cultural aspects. Prior study and preparation will help you make or avoid contact if you have to deal with the local population. People will be friendly, unfriendly, or they will choose to ignore you. Their attitude may be unknown. If the people are known to be friendly, try to keep them friendly through your courtesy and respect for their religion, politics, social customs, habits, and all other aspects of their culture. If the people are known to be enemies or are unknowns, make every effort to avoid any contact and leave no sign of your presence. A basic knowledge of the daily habits of the local people will be essential in this attempt. If after careful observation you determine that an unknown people are friendly, you may contact them if you absolutely need their help. Usually, you have little to fear and much to gain from cautious and respectful contact with local people of friendly or neutral countries. If you become familiar with the local customs, display common decency, and most important, show respect for their customs, you should be able to avoid trouble and possibly gain needed help. To make contact, wait until only one person is near and, if possible, let that person make the initial approach. Most people will be willing to help a survivor who appears to be in need. However, local political attitudes, instruction, or propaganda efforts may change the attitudes of otherwise friendly people. Conversely, in unfriendly countries, many people, especially in remote areas, may feel animosity toward their politicians and may be more friendly toward a survivor.

The key to successful contact with local peoples is to be friendly, courteous, and patient. Displaying fear, showing weapons, and making sudden or threatening movements can cause a local person to fear you. Such actions can prompt a hostile response. When attempting a contact, smile as often as you can. Many local peoples are shy and seem unapproachable, or they may ignore you. Approach them slowly and do not rush your contact.

SELF DEFENSE IN ECONOMIC COLLAPSE

In all likelihood, during an economic collapse, your life and the life of your loved ones will be at risk. You may not have any weapon available to you because you never legally purchased one or it is because you hate weapons all together. In such case, you have to be able to use your bare hands and feet for protection. You will have practiced before these techniques so that you can use them. The amount of techniques that you learn should be limited and you should spend considerable time on mastering them. It is good to have a rooted foundation in the basics of fighting. Martial arts and the perfection of it is a serious study which should be taken seriously so that if you are in the unfortunate situation where you may be killed, you can defend yourself.

The core of fighting is:

- Punching Opponent (Boxing)
- Kicking Opponent (Karate, Taekwondo, Muay Thai)
- Throwing Opponent (Judo)
- Standing grappling (Judo, Wrestling)
- Ground grappling (Wrestling, Jujitsu)
- Submissions (Jujitsu, Catch Wrestling)

Training in a combination of various styles techniques is known as Mixed Martial Arts or MMA. The point is to stay alive, not compare dojo appreciation badges. In a gym, martial arts school, dojo, or training center, your sparring with the opponent is muted. You do not attempt to kill the opponent. You are sparring to gain experience and to practice the techniques that you have been studying.

During an economic collapse, you may be attacked by individuals that seek to rob you or murder you or even worse. You can have no mercy, in being able to defend yourself, in such a life threatening time as an economic collapse. You must strike harder, faster, and with greater speed than you have before. You don't have time for complex 7 step submission routines. You have to take out your opponent using your bare hands and feet with blazing speed. Your opponent, contrary to what would happen during a civil society, may have no mercy on you. He or she may seek to kill you to take your resources. The point of self-defense is NOT to hurt your opponent. The point is self-defense is to prevent you getting hurt. In Karate, the principle of "No First Attack" is a vital element in the training regimen of the 50 million Karate practitioners on earth. You should follow the same principle of "No First Attack". Self-defense techniques, whether in one style or various styles, should be practiced regularly so that is can help you when in a time of danger. A basic principle of martial arts is to use the opponent's strength and momentum against him to gain more leverage than one's own muscles alone can generate, thereby gaining an advantage. In close combat, you must exploit every advantage over an opponent to ensure a successful outcome. This can include employing various close combat techniques that will present a dilemma to an opponent. Achieving surprise can also greatly increase leverage.

Speed

Using speed to gain the initiative and advantage over the enemy. In close combat, the speed and violence of the attack against an opponent provides you with a distinct advantage. You must know and understand the basics of close combat so they can act instinctively with speed to execute close combat techniques.

Adapting

Close combat can be characterized by friction, uncertainty, disorder, and rapid change. Each situation is a unique combination of shifting factors that cannot be controlled with precision or certainty. If you adapt quickly you will have a significant advantage.

Verbal Self Defense

Verbal self-defense is the process of using voice commands to create barriers that protect you. If for example, an individual becomes close to you to attack;

You should:

1. Warn them to keep distance from you

2. If they approach closer, issue a 2nd warning that you will defend yourself. If they continue approaching.

3. If individual keeps approaching, you have to defend yourself using whatever capability you have available to you. If individual complies and keeps distance, then you can continue verbal engagement.

The overall rule of self-defense is to use only as much force as needed to defend yourself. It is defense, not offense. The point of self-defense is not to destroy your opponent. The point of self-defense is defense and survival. Bear in mind that during such a critical time as an economic collapse, other people may not have the same rule of engagement as you. They may seek to murder and steal from other's in order to get their resources. This is

why in your attack you should be able to determine beforehand the type of person you are dealing with and they thieves that may or not be armed. These are people that are seeking resources because they have either ran out or are just seeking more resources. You have to decide based on the signs that are presented, if the person seeking to steal from you is dangerous or if they are just hungry.
An enemy will not normally surrender because he is placed at a disadvantage. You cannot be satisfied with gaining an advantage in a close combat situation. You must exploit any advantage aggressively and ruthlessly until an opportunity arises to completely dominate the opponent. You must exploit success by using every advantage that can be gained.

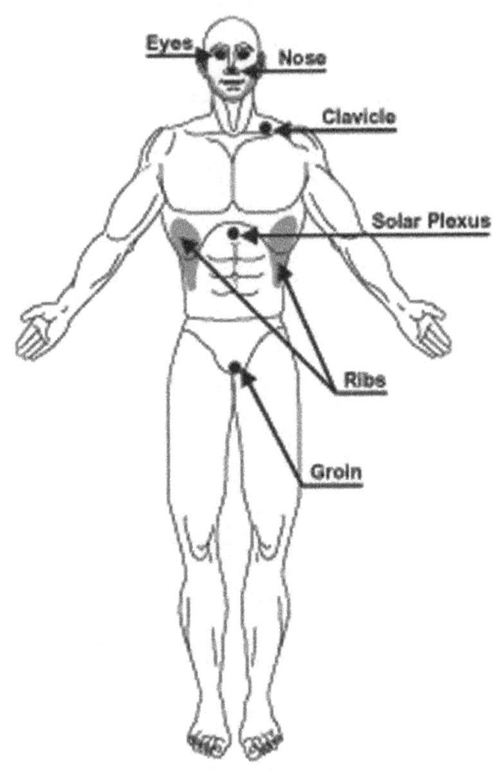
Eyes
Nose
Clavicle
Solar Plexus
Ribs
Groin

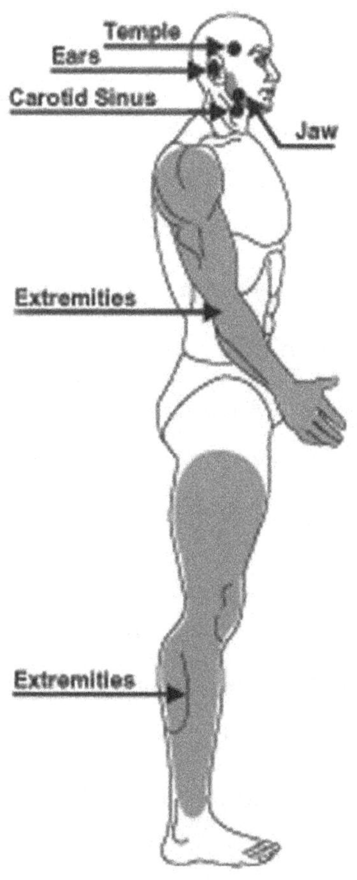

Vital Parts of the body to strike include the eyes, nose, ribs, groin, solar plexus, clavicle, ears, jaw, carotid sinus, and temple.

POWERFUL SELF-DEFENSE WEAPONS

- **Kicks** – The strongest weapon you have and it is your most powerful weapon, if trained correctly in its application.

- **Knees** – Knee strikes, when delivered with precision, are highly painful and damaging to your opponent. Just a few knee strikes could incapacitate your opponent, sending him wobbling off.

- **Elbows** – The elbows are among the hardest bones in your body. They are natural striking tools and can be used in combination with a hook punch.

- **Fists** – Your fists are time tested natural weapons that can devastate your opponent in a short time. Practice punching often and train like you are fighting.

- **Voice** – Use your voice and reasonable language to defuse a conflict before it takes place. Many conflicts could have been avoided if just one of the conflict had communicated.

ATTACK TARGETS

- Head - The vulnerable regions of the head are the eyes, temple, nose, ears, and jaw. Massive damage to the head kills an opponent.

- Eyes - The eyes are excellent targets because they are soft tissue areas that are not protected by bone or muscle. Attacks to this area may cause the opponent to protect the area with his hands, allowing you to execute a secondary attack to other target areas while the opponent uses his hands to protect his eyes.

- Temple - The temple is one of the most fragile areas of the head. Powerful strikes to the opponent's temple cause permanent damage and death.

- Nose - The nose is very sensitive and easily broken. An attack to this area causes involuntary watering and closing of the opponent's eyes, rendering him vulnerable to secondary attacks. However, through training, individuals can condition themselves to withstand attacks to the nose. Therefore, any attack to the nose must be powerfully delivered.

- Ears - Attacks to the ears may cause the eardrum to rupture. But this may not stop or even distract an opponent unless you powerfully deliver the strike.

- Jaw - The jaw region, when struck forcefully, renders the opponent unconscious. Strikes to the jaw cause painful injuries to the teeth and surrounding tissues (e.g., lips, tongue), but the risk of self-injury is great unless you deliver strikes with a hard object.

- Neck - The front of the neck, or throat area, is a soft tissue area that is not covered by natural protection. Damage to this region causes the opponent's trachea to swell, closing his airway, which can lead to death.

- Carotid Sinus - The carotid sinus is located on both sides of the neck just below the jaw. Strikes to the carotid sinus restrict blood flow to the brain, causing loss of consciousness or death.

- Cervical Vertebrae - The cervical vertebrae on the back of the neck, from the base of the skull to the top of the shoulders, contains the spinal cord, which is the nervous system's link to the brain. The weight of the head and the lack of large muscle mass allow damage to the cervical vertebrae and spinal cord. Excessive damage to this area causes pain, paralysis, or death.

- Clavicle - The opponent's clavicle (or collar bone) can be easily fractured, causing immobilization of the arm.

- Solar Plexus. Attacks to the opponent's solar plexus or center of the chest can knock the breath out of him and immobilize him.

- Ribs. Damage to the opponent's ribs immobilizes him. It may also cause internal trauma.

- Kidneys. Powerful attacks to the opponent's kidneys cause immobilization, permanent damage, or death.

- Groin - The groin area is another soft tissue area not covered by natural protection. Any damage to this area causes the opponent to involuntarily protect his injured area, usually with his hands or legs.

ANIMAL TRACKING

- If you are tracking an animal at night, you should use a flashlight to assist you.

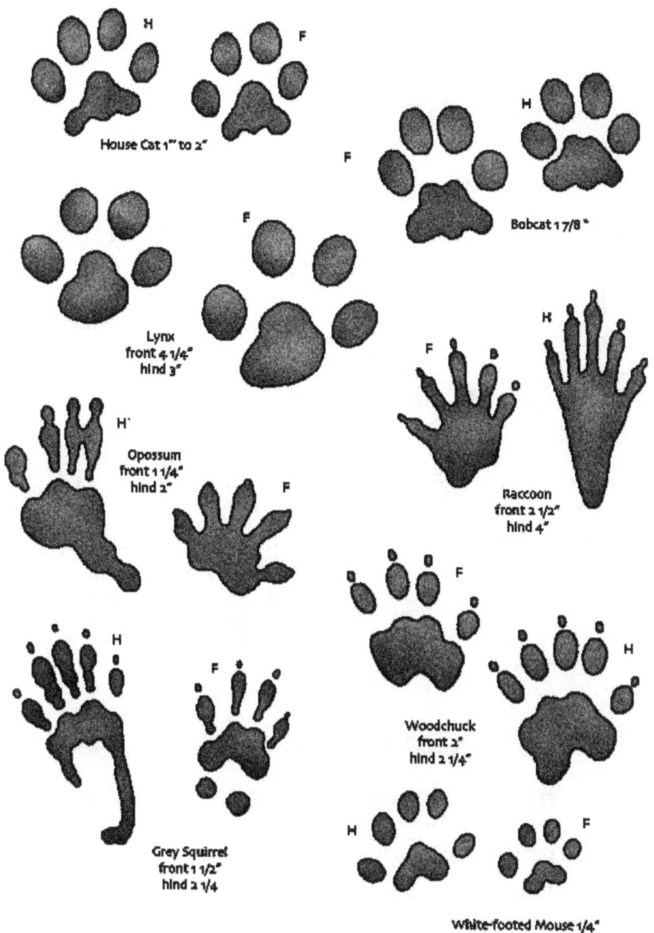

- Constantly look for signs that can tell you if the animal you are tracking has been in this direction or area previously.

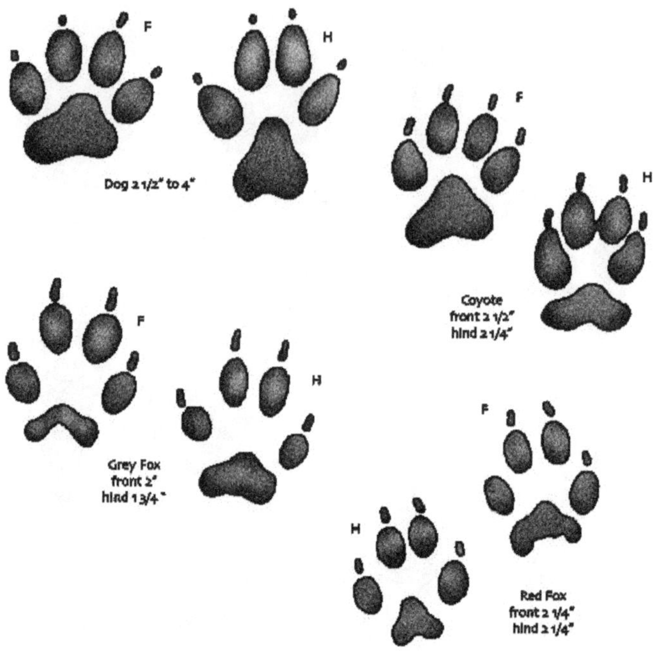

- You should make every attempt to be as quiet as possible so as to not scare the animal you are tracking.

- Use the charts listed below and above in order to match the footprint of the animal you are tracking.

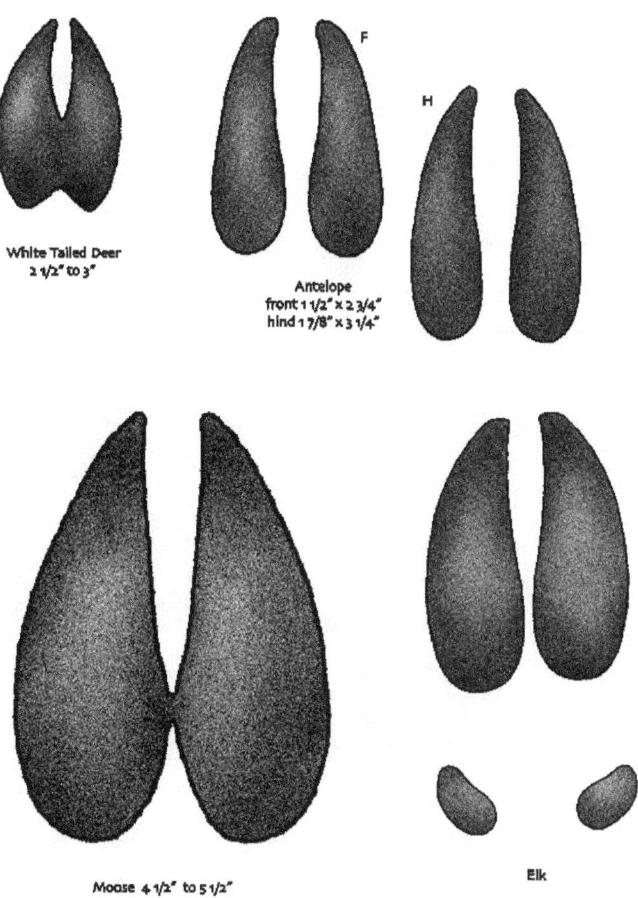

- Soft mud reveals animal tracks much easier than dirt or baked earth.

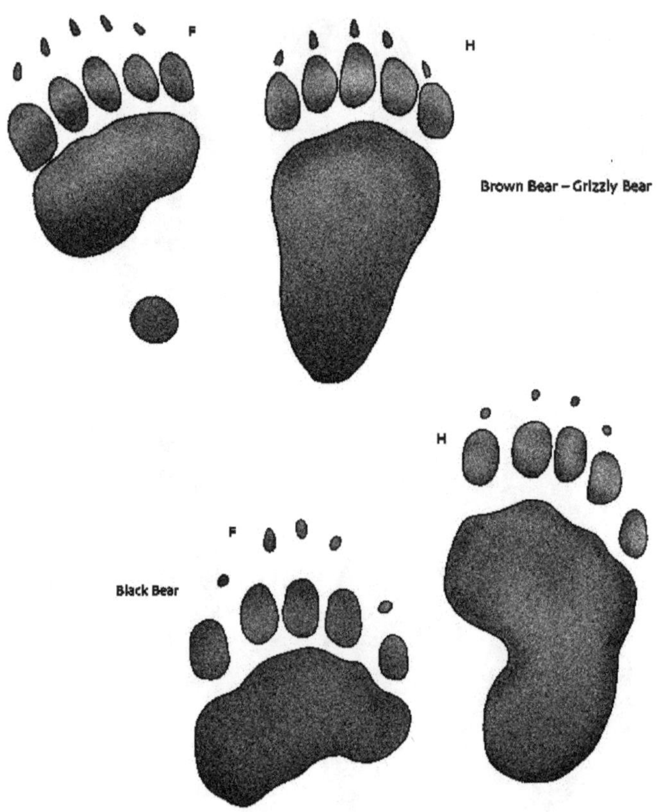
F
H
Brown Bear – Grizzly Bear
H
F
Black Bear

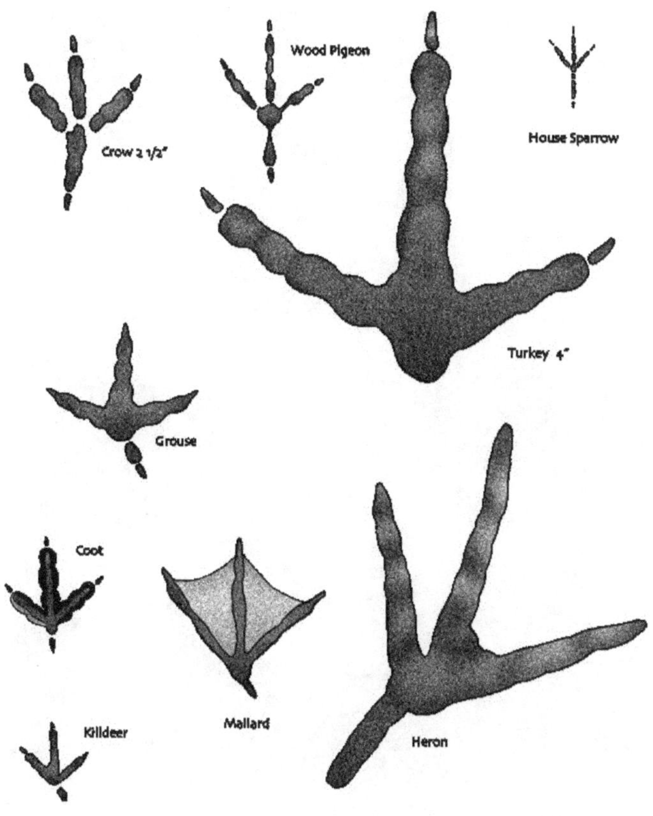
Wood Pigeon
House Sparrow
Crow 2 1/2"
Turkey 4"
Grouse
Coot
Killdeer
Mallard
Heron

CHARACTER	*MORSE CODE*	*TELEPHONY*	*PHONIC (PRONUNCIATION)*
A	• —	Alfa	(AL-FAH)
B	— • • •	Bravo	(BRAH-VOH)
C	— • — •	Charlie	(CHAR-LEE) or (SHAR-LEE)
D	— • •	Delta	(DELL-TAH)
E	•	Echo	(ECK-OH)
F	• • — •	Foxtrot	(FOKS-TROT)
G	— — •	Golf	(GOLF)
H	• • • •	Hotel	(HOH-TEL)
I	• •	India	(IN-DEE-AH)
J	• — — —	Juliett	(JEW-LEE-ETT)
K	— • —	Kilo	(KEY-LOH)
L	• — • •	Lima	(LEE-MAH)
M	— —	Mike	(MIKE)
N	— •	November	(NO-VEM-BER)
O	— — —	Oscar	(OSS-CAH)
P	• — — •	Papa	(PAH-PAH)
Q	— — • —	Quebec	(KEH-BECK)
R	• — •	Romeo	(ROW-ME-OH)
S	• • •	Sierra	(SEE-AIR-RAH)
T	—	Tango	(TANG-GO)
U	• • —	Uniform	(YOU-NEE-FORM) or (OO-NEE-FORM)
V	• • • —	Victor	(VIK-TAH)
W	• — —	Whiskey	(WISS-KEY)
X	— • • —	Xray	(ECKS-RAY)
Y	— • — —	Yankee	(YANG-KEY)
Z	— — • •	Zulu	(ZOO-LOO)
1	• — — — —	One	(WUN)
2	• • — — —	Two	(TOO)
3	• • • — —	Three	(TREE)
4	• • • • —	Four	(FOW-ER)
5	• • • • •	Five	(FIFE)
6	— • • • •	Six	(SIX)
7	— — • • •	Seven	(SEV-EN)
8	— — — • •	Eight	(AIT)
9	— — — — •	Nine	(NIN-ER)
0	— — — — —	Zero	(ZEE-RO)

THE NATIVE AMERICAN CREED

(1) One Supreme Spirit

(2) Immortality of the soul

(3) Sacredness of body

(4) Asceticism – Less consumption

(5) Respect for Elders

(6) Property is sacred. Theft is non-existent.

(7) Eye for an Eye

(8) Cleanliness

(9) Purity of morals.

(10) Truth

(11) Beautification of environment

(12) Collectivism and simple life

13) Hospitality and that visitor is sacred.

(14) Courage

(15) Life without regret

RULES OF THE TEEPEE

- Be hospitable.
- Always assume that your guest is tired, cold, and hungry.
- Always give your guest the place of honor in the lodge and at the feast, and serve him in reasonable ways.
- Never sit while your guest stands.
- Go hungry rather than stint your guest.
- If your guest refuses certain food, say nothing; he may be under vow.
- Protect your guest as one of the family; feed his horse, and beat your dogs if they harm his dog.
- Do not trouble your guest with many questions about himself; he will tell you what he wishes you to know.
- In another man's lodge follow his customs, not your own.

- Never worry your host with your troubles.
- Always repay calls of courtesy.
- Give your host a little present on leaving; little presents are little courtesies and never give offence.
- Say "Thank you" for every gift, however small.
- Compliment your host, even if you strain the facts to do so.
- Never walk between persons talking.
- Never interrupt persons talking.
- Let not the young speak among those much older, unless asked.
- Always give place to your seniors in entering or leaving the lodge; or anywhere.
- Never sit while your seniors stand.
- Never force your conversation on any one.

- Speak softly, especially before your elders, or in presence of strangers.
- Never come between anyone & the fire.
- Do not touch live coals with a steel knife or any sharp steel.
- Do not stare at strangers; drop your eyes if they stare hard at you.
- The women of the lodge are the keepers of the fire, but the men should help with the heavier sticks.
- Always give a word or sign of salute when meeting or passing a friend, or even a stranger, if in a lonely place.
- Do not talk to your mother-in-law at any time, or let her talk to you.
- Be kind.
- Show respect to all men, but grovel to none.
- Let silence be your motto till duty bids you

THE LAST WORD

The economic collapse may happen or may not happen in your lifetime. What is important is if you have read this book thoroughly, you should have a basic understanding of what it will take for you to survive an actual economic collapse. No one can predict with any degree of certainty what will happen to local and international economies in the future. Everyone's guess is just as good as your guess. But there are steps that you can take today to ensure that your future will be secure if indeed such an economic collapse occurs. The old adage of “Better safe than sorry” never rang so true. It is better to be prepared and to have your family prepared. Thank you for reading my book. Please share the knowledge.

Sincerely,

Kambiz Mostofizadeh

UNITED STATES BILL OF RIGHTS

Amendment I

Congress shall make no law respecting an establishment of religion, or prohibiting the free exercise thereof; or abridging the freedom of speech, or of the press; or the right of the people peaceably to assemble, and to petition the Government for a redress of grievances.

Amendment II

A well-regulated Militia, being necessary to the security of a free State, the right of the people to keep and bear Arms, shall not be infringed.

Amendment III

No Soldier shall, in time of peace be quartered in any house, without the consent of the Owner, nor in time of war, but in a manner to be prescribed by law.

Amendment IV

The right of the people to be secure in their persons, houses, papers, and effects, against unreasonable searches and seizures, shall not be violated, and no Warrants shall issue, but upon probable cause, supported by Oath or affirmation, and particularly describing the place to be searched, and the persons or things to be seized.

Amendment V

No person shall be held to answer for a capital, or otherwise infamous crime, unless on a presentment or indictment of a Grand Jury, except in cases arising in the land or naval forces, or in the Militia, when in actual service in time of War or public danger; nor shall any person be subject for the same offence to be twice put in jeopardy of life or limb; nor shall be compelled in any criminal case to be a witness against himself, nor be deprived of life, liberty, or property, without due process of law; nor shall private property be taken for public use, without just compensation.

Amendment VI

In all criminal prosecutions, the accused shall enjoy the right to a speedy and public trial, by an impartial jury of the State and district wherein the crime shall have been committed, which district shall have been previously ascertained by law, and to be informed of the nature and cause of the accusation; to be confronted with the witnesses against him; to have compulsory process for obtaining witnesses in his favor, and to have the Assistance of Counsel for his defense.

Amendment VII

In Suits at common law, where the value in controversy shall exceed twenty dollars, the right of trial by jury shall be preserved, and no fact tried by a jury, shall be otherwise re-examined in any Court of the United States, than according to the rules of the common law.

Amendment VIII

Excessive bail shall not be required, nor excessive fines imposed, nor cruel and unusual punishments inflicted.

Amendment IX

The enumeration in the Constitution, of certain rights, shall not be construed to deny or disparage others retained by the people.

Amendment X

The powers not delegated to the United States by the Constitution, nor prohibited by it to the States, are reserved to the States respectively, or to the people.

NOTES

NOTES

NOTES

NOTES

NOTES

NOTES

NOTES

NOTES

NOTES

NOTES

NOTES

NOTES

NOTES

NOTES

NOTES

NOTES

NOTES

NOTES

www.ingramcontent.com/pod-product-compliance
Lightning Source LLC
Chambersburg PA
CBHW032005190326
41520CB00007B/360
9781942825050